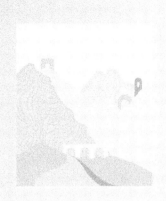   

FASZINIERENDE LANDSCHAFTEN

Malbuch zur Entspannung und zum Stressabbau

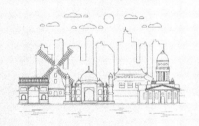 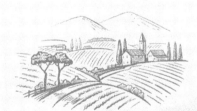

Nature & Art Editions

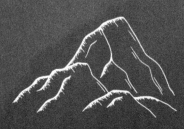

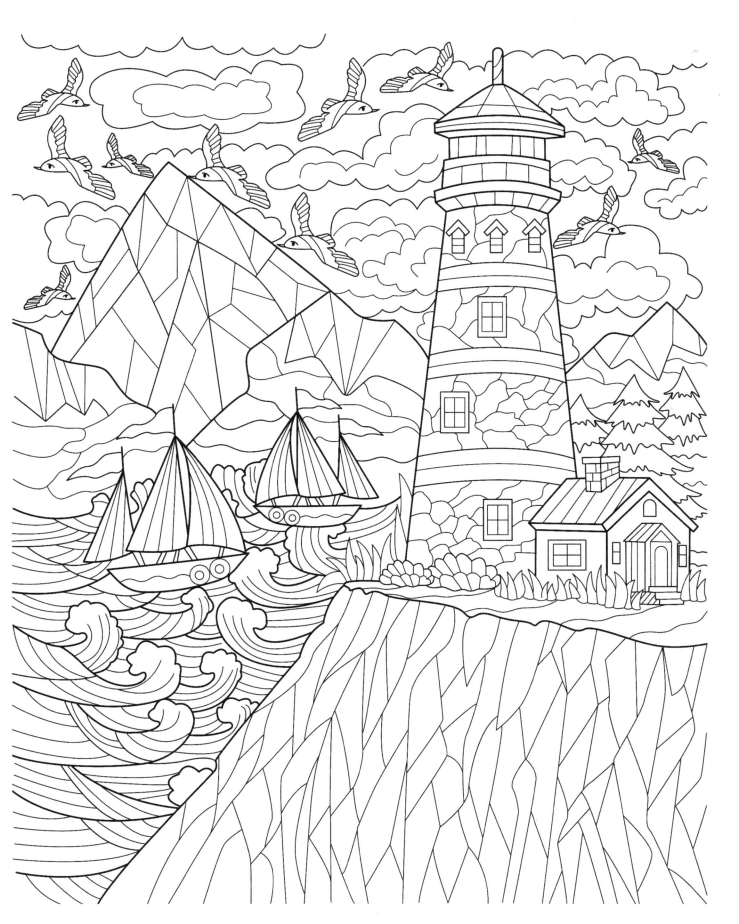

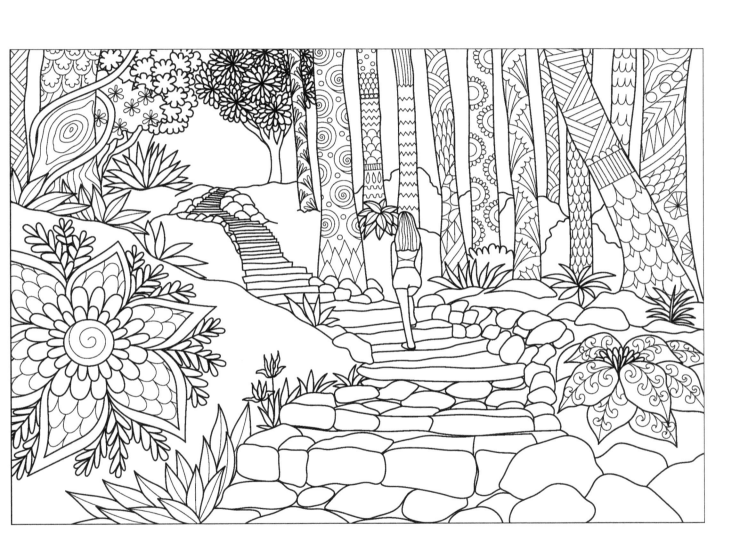

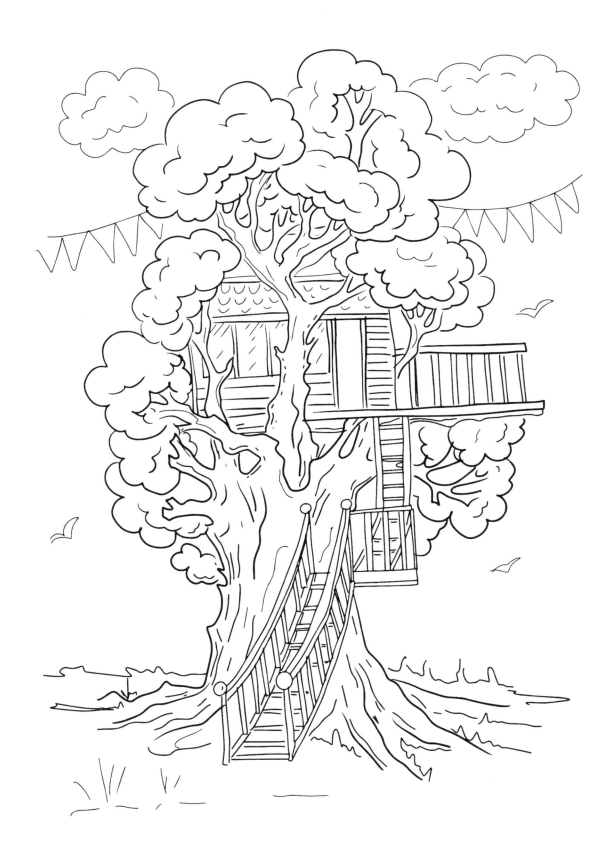

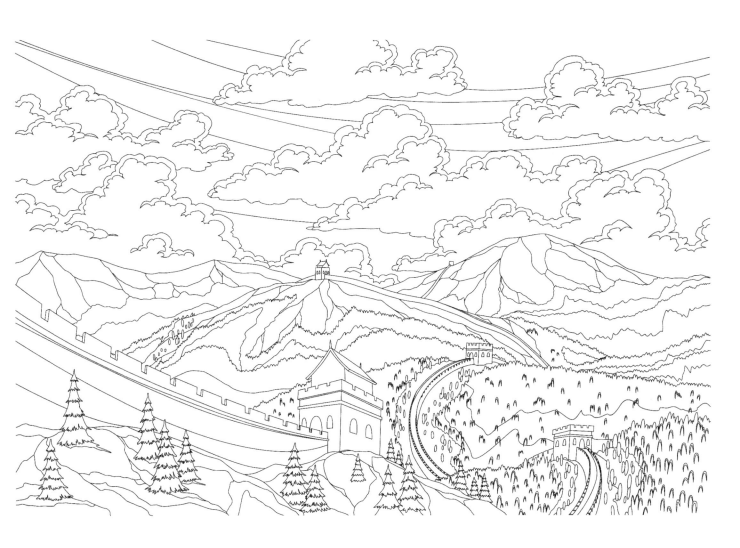

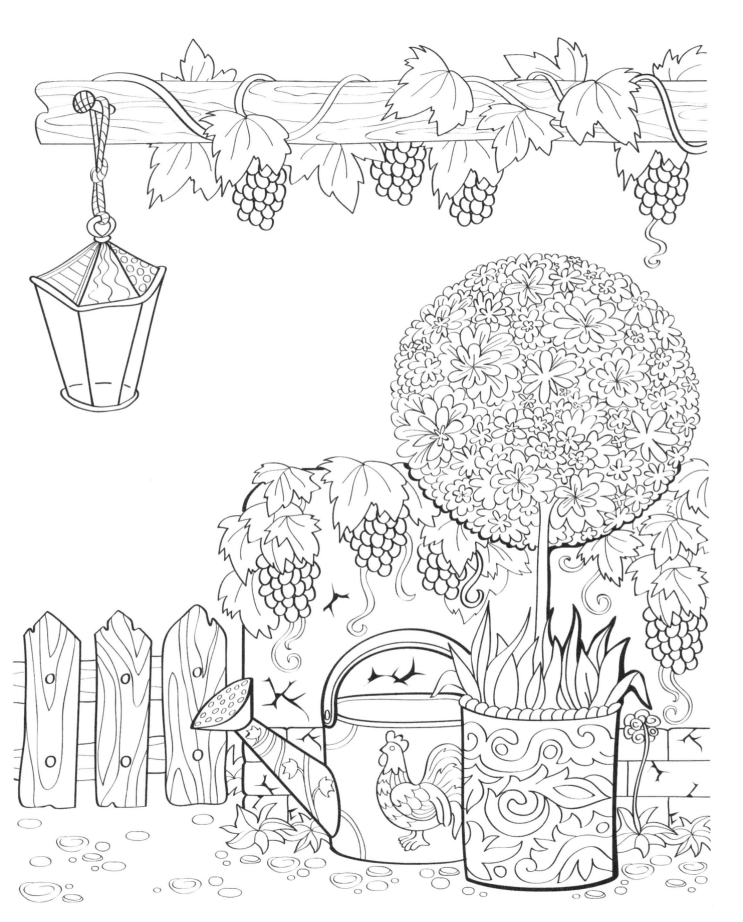

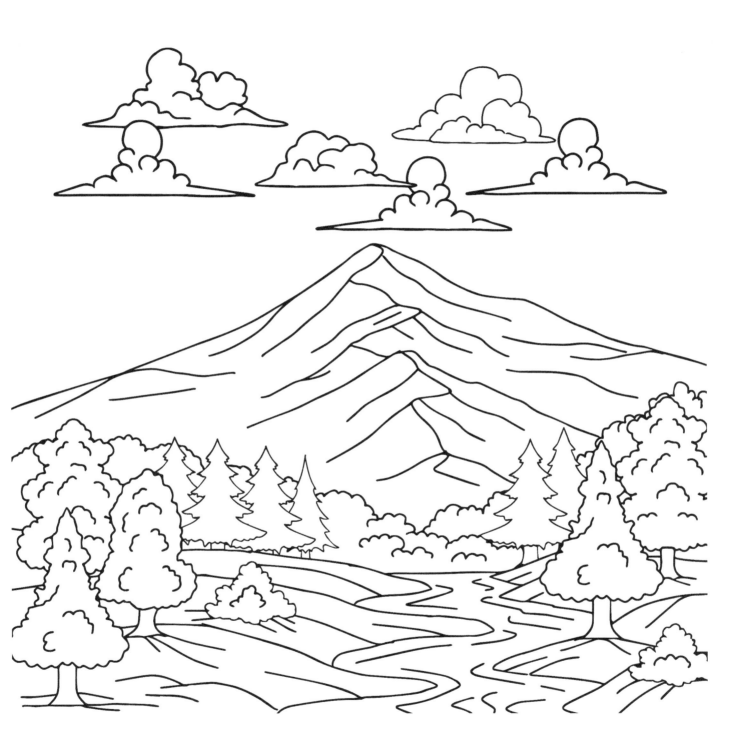

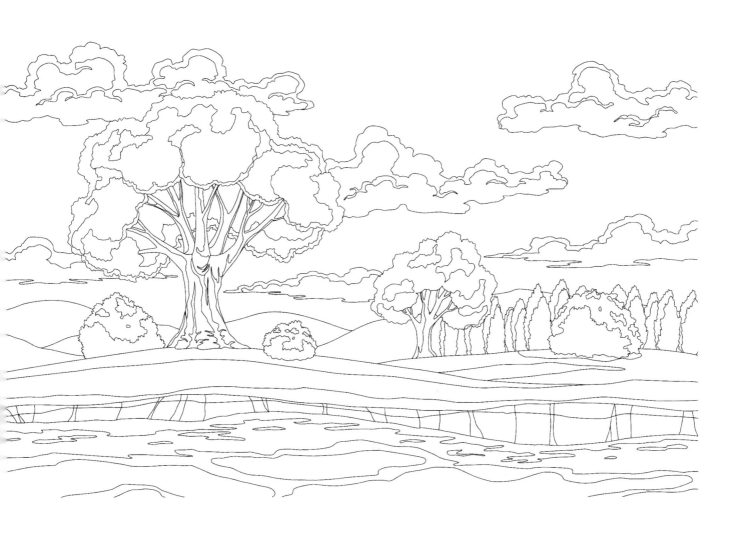

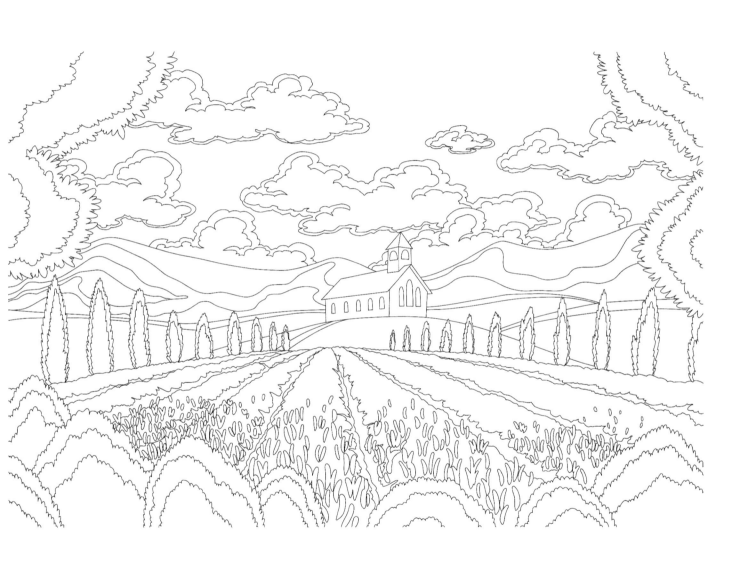

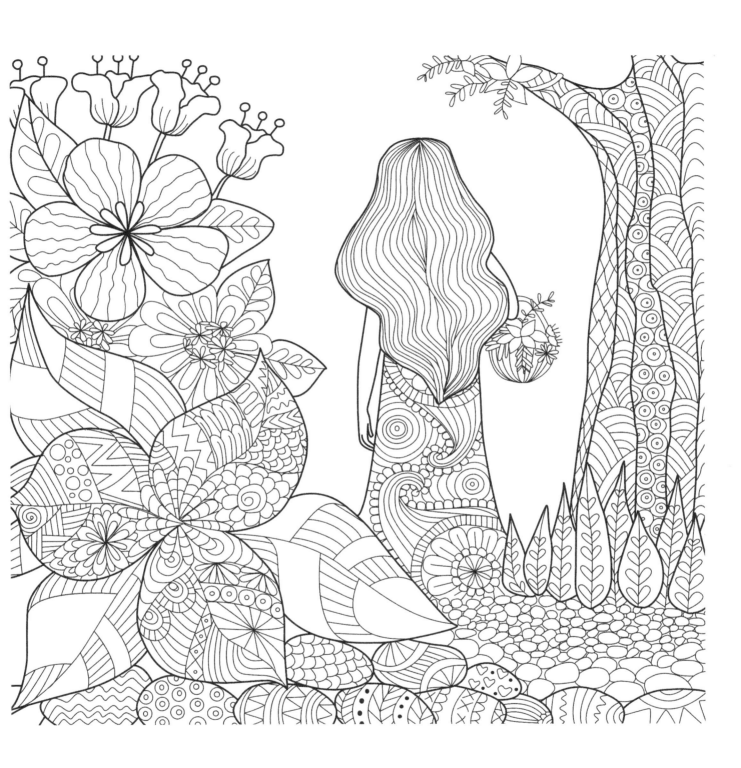

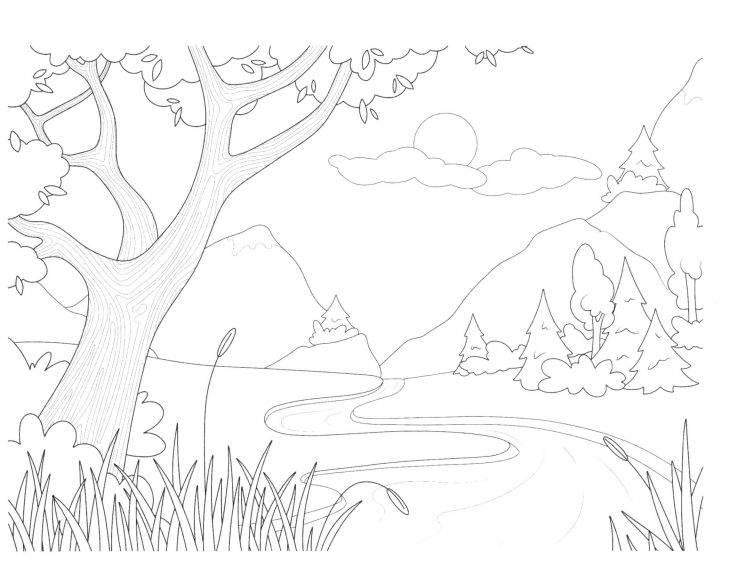

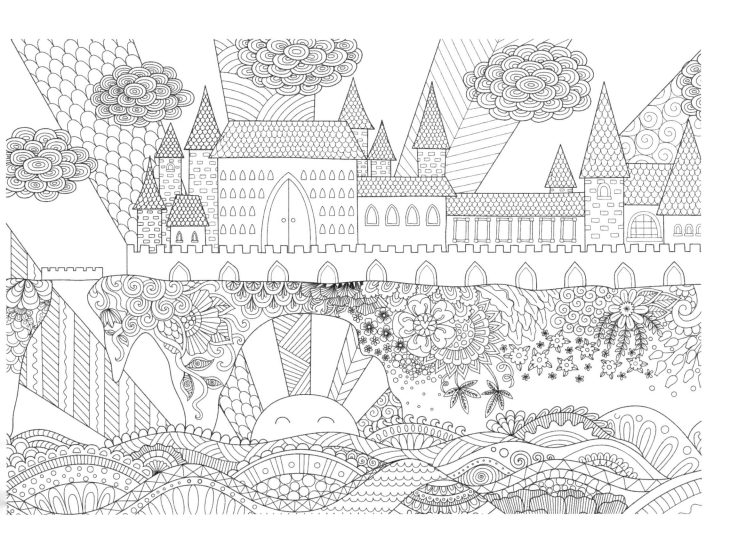

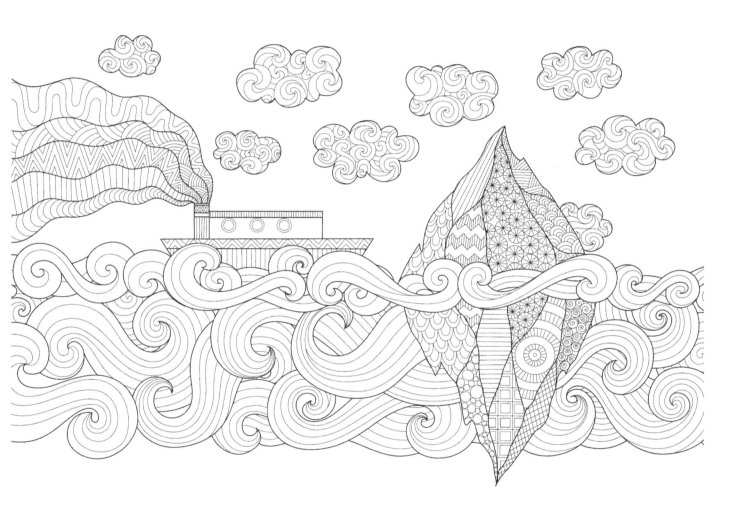

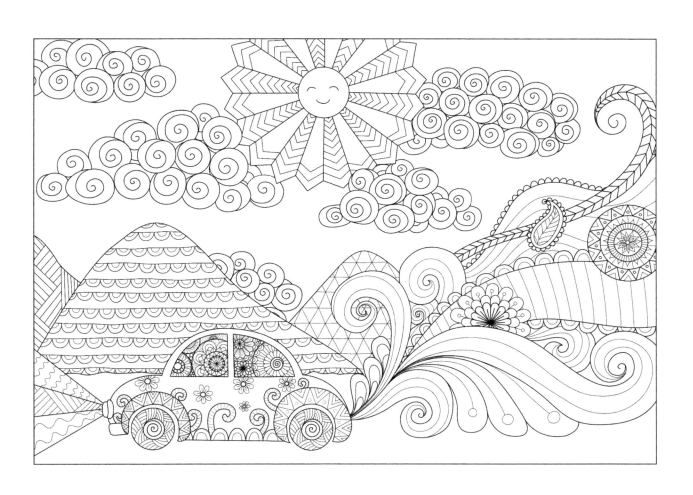

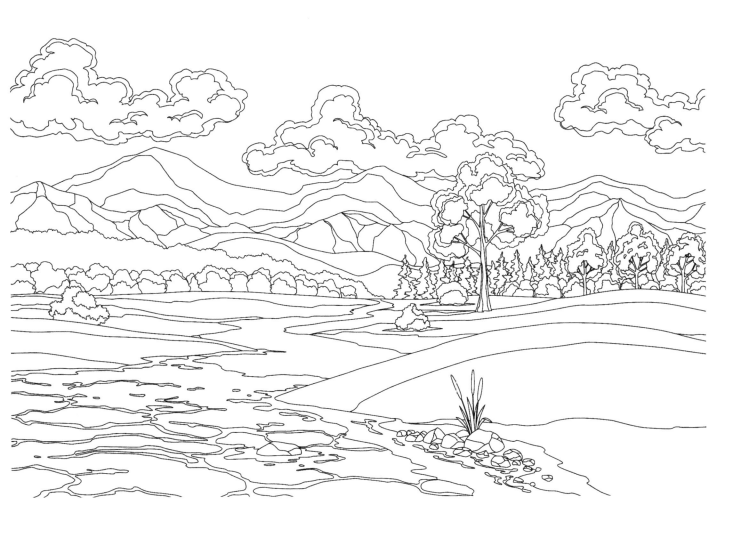

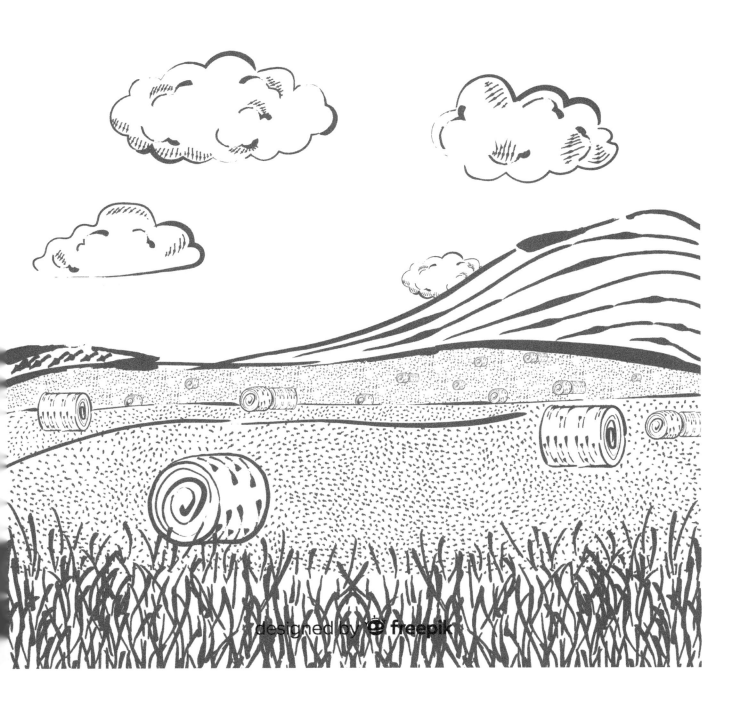

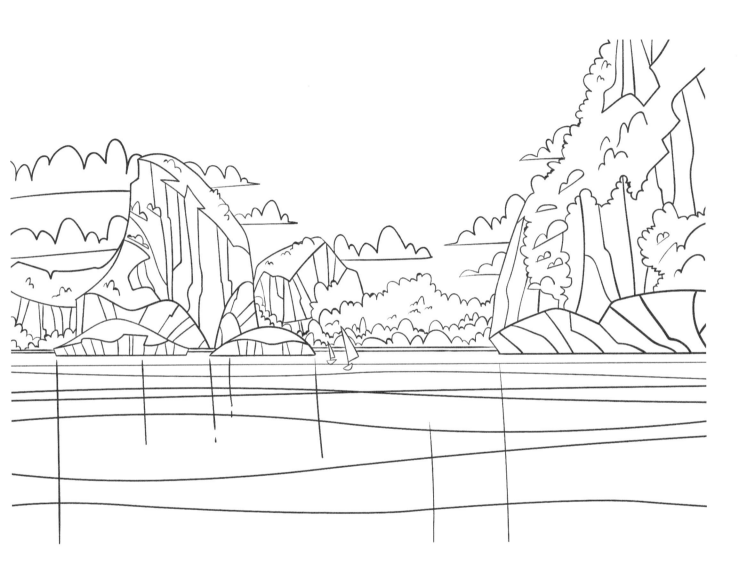

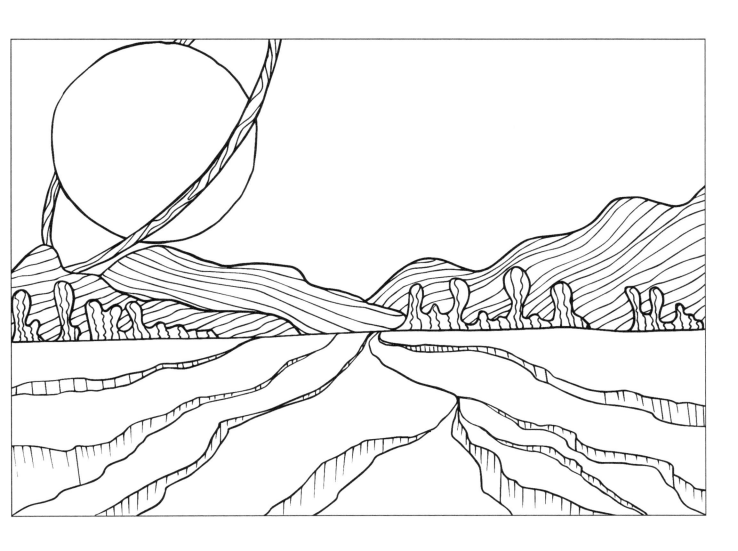

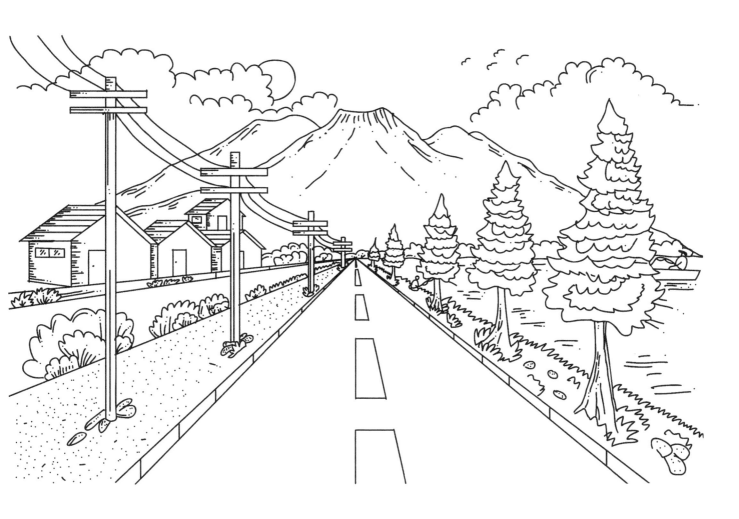

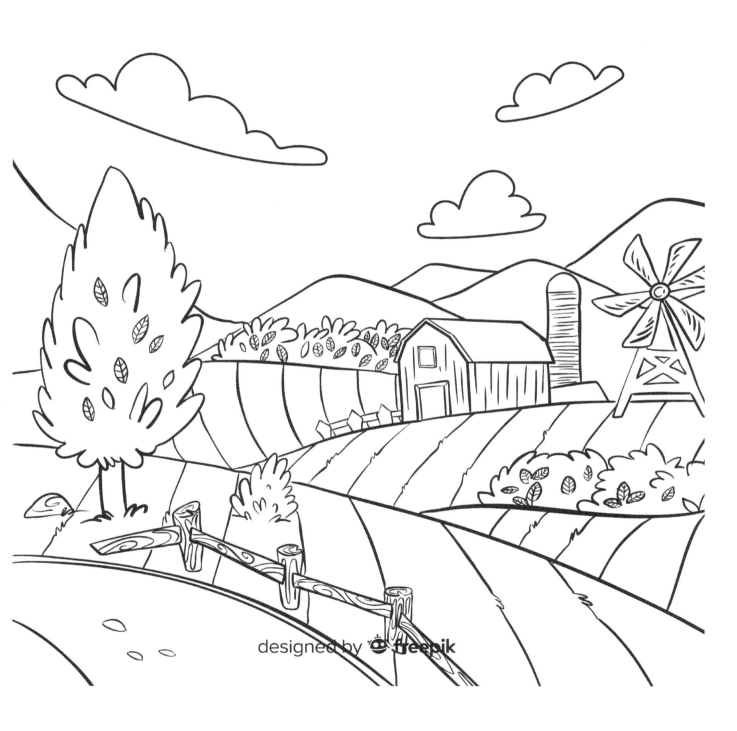

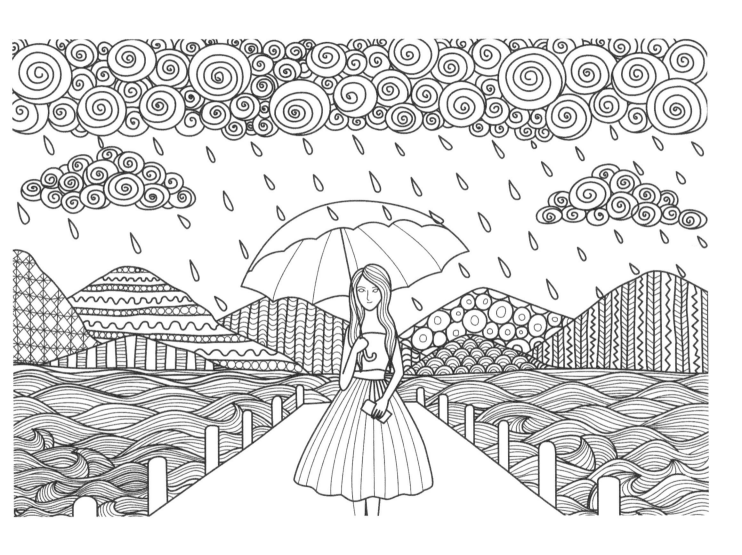

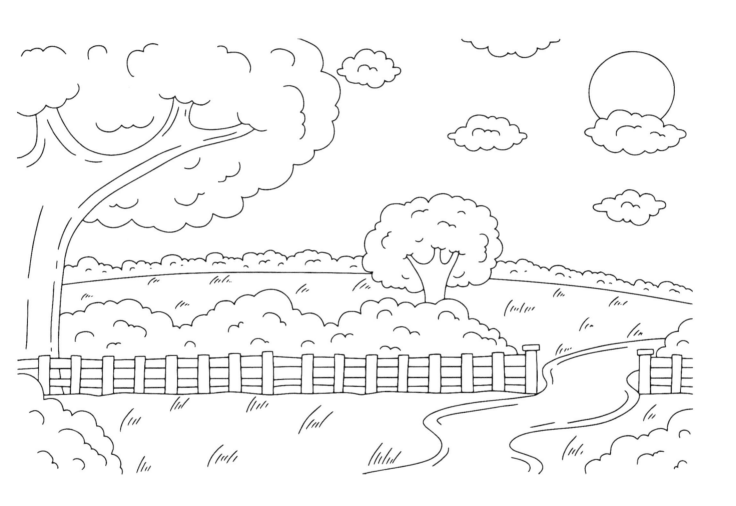

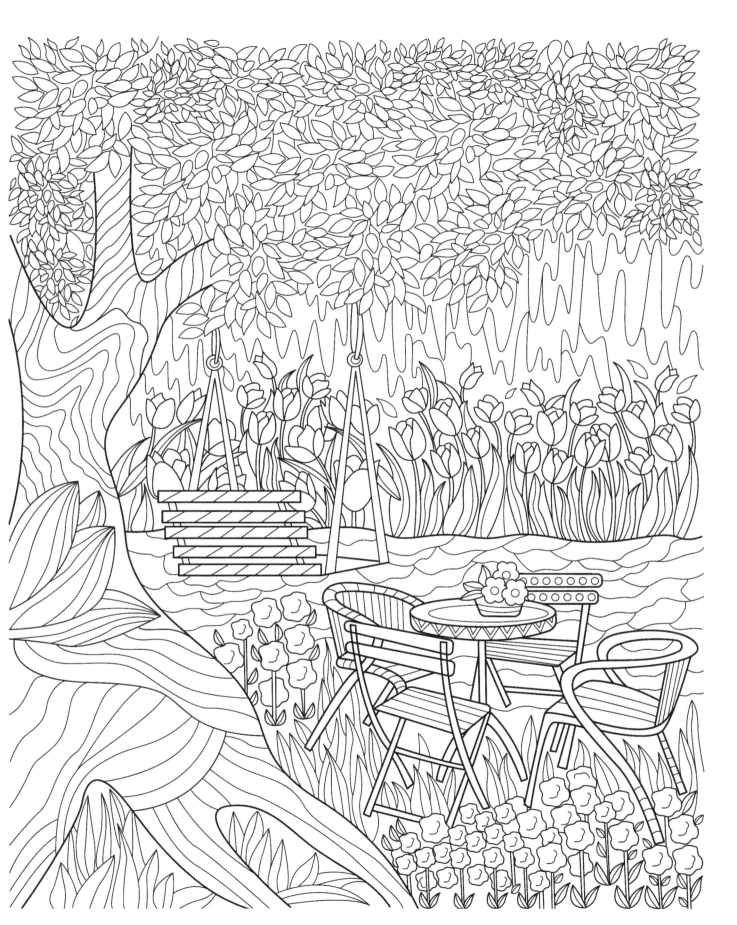

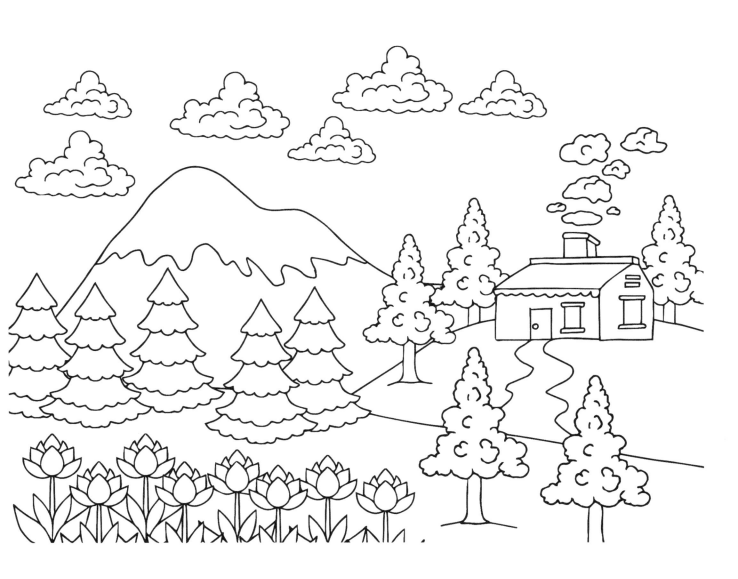

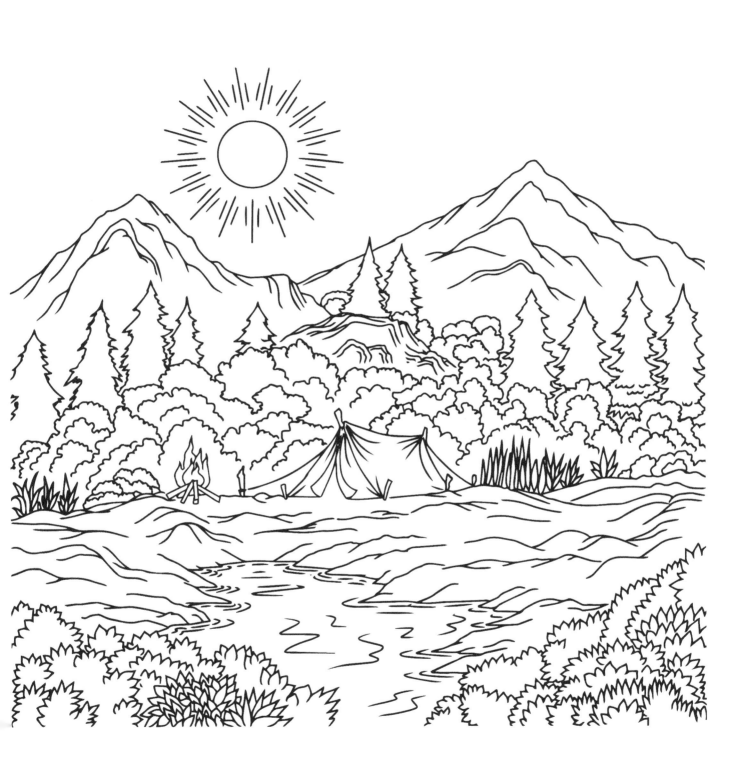

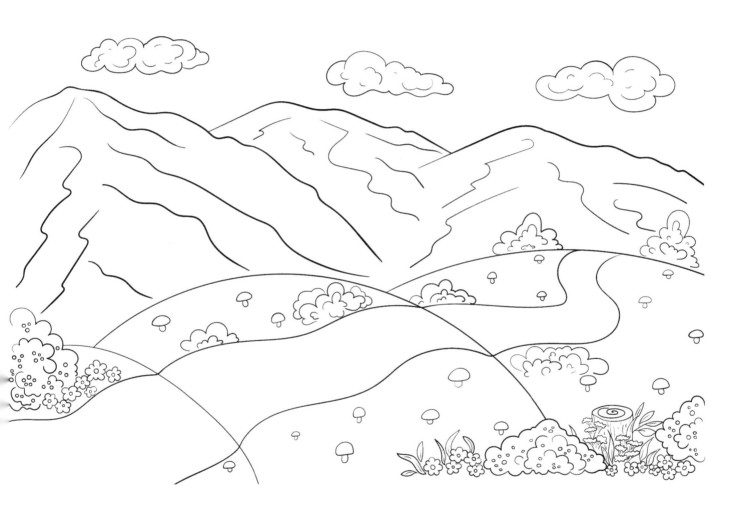

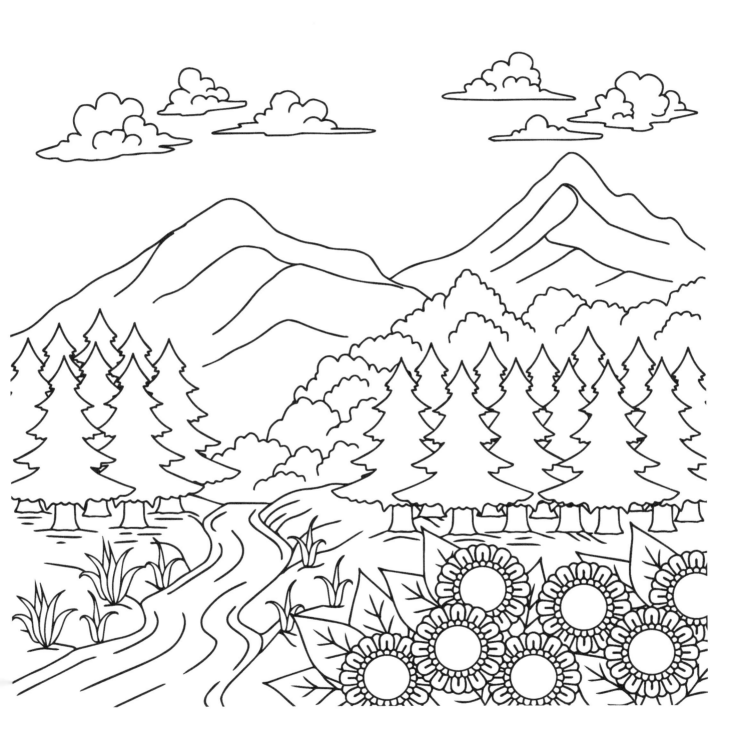

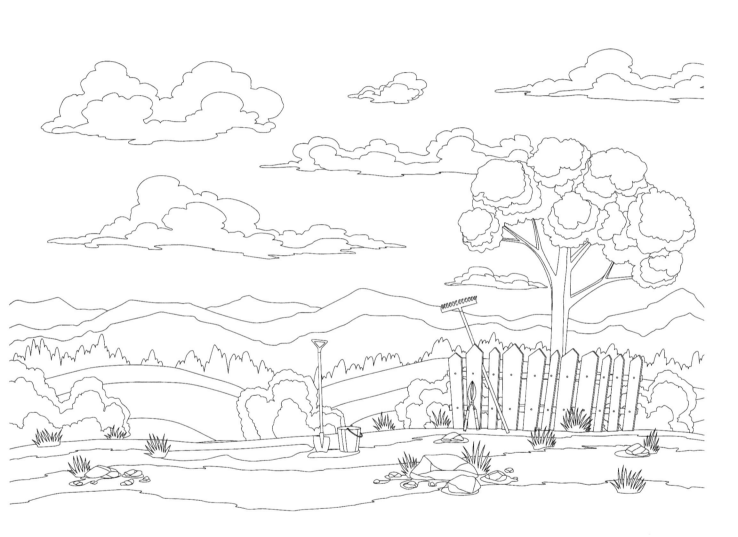

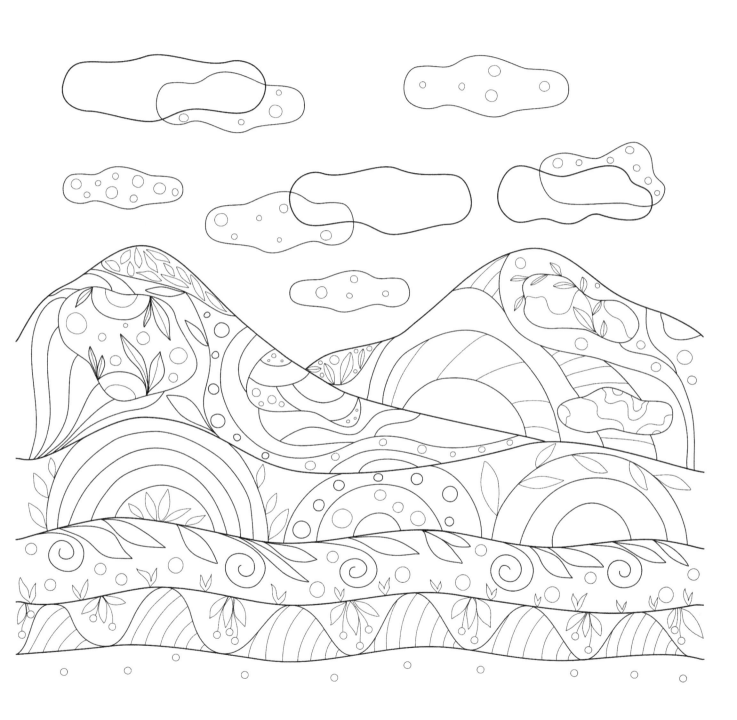

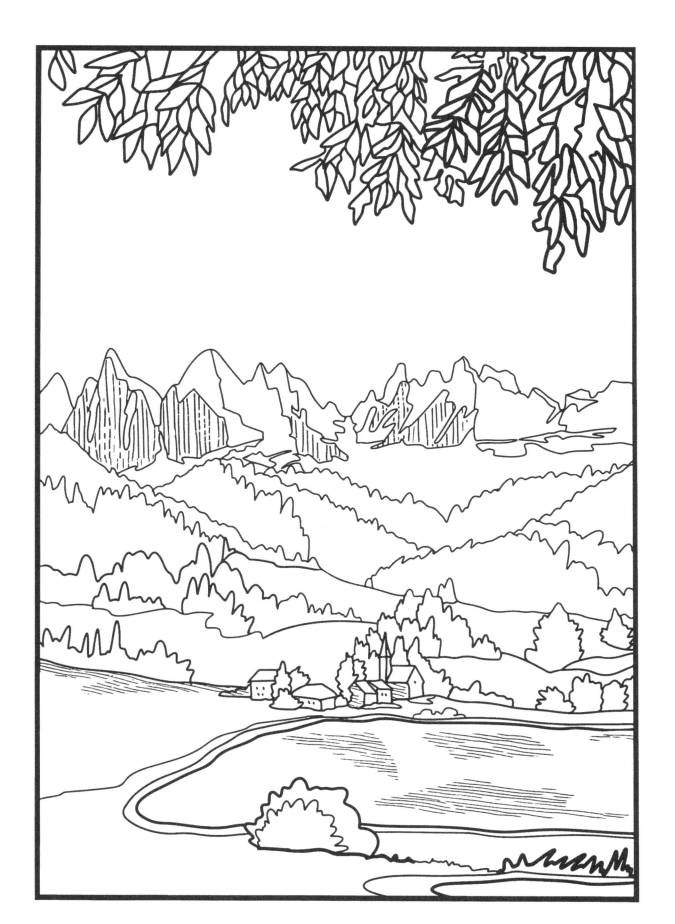

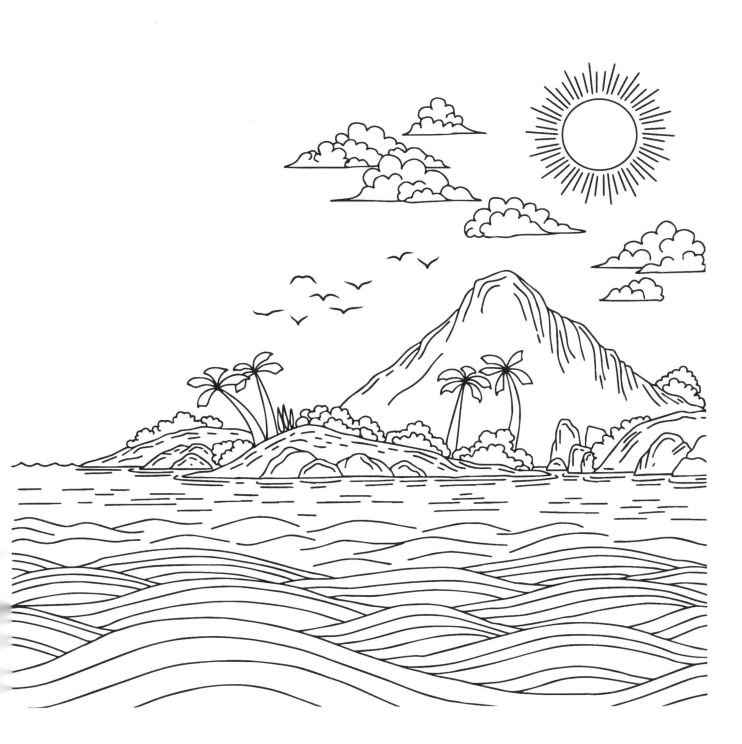

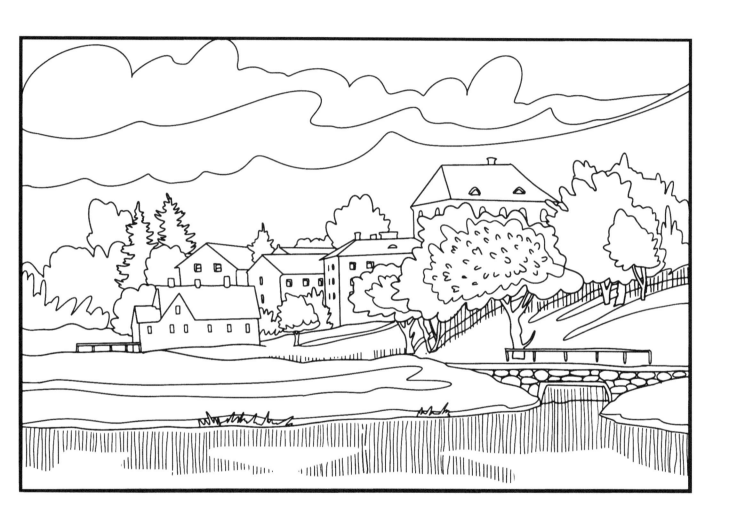

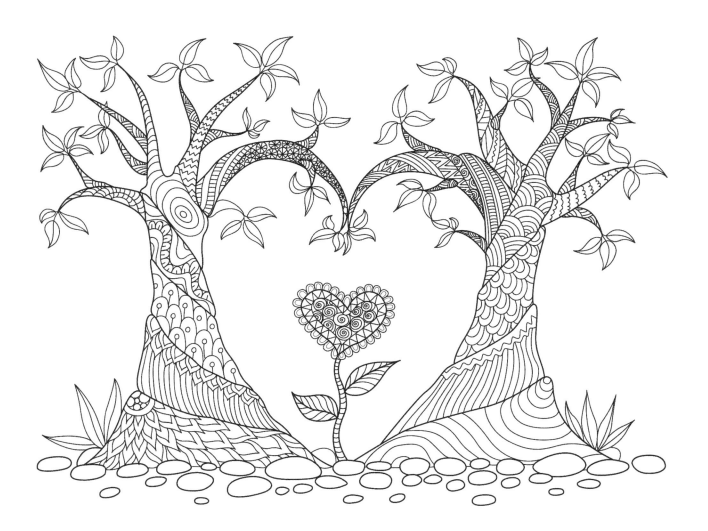

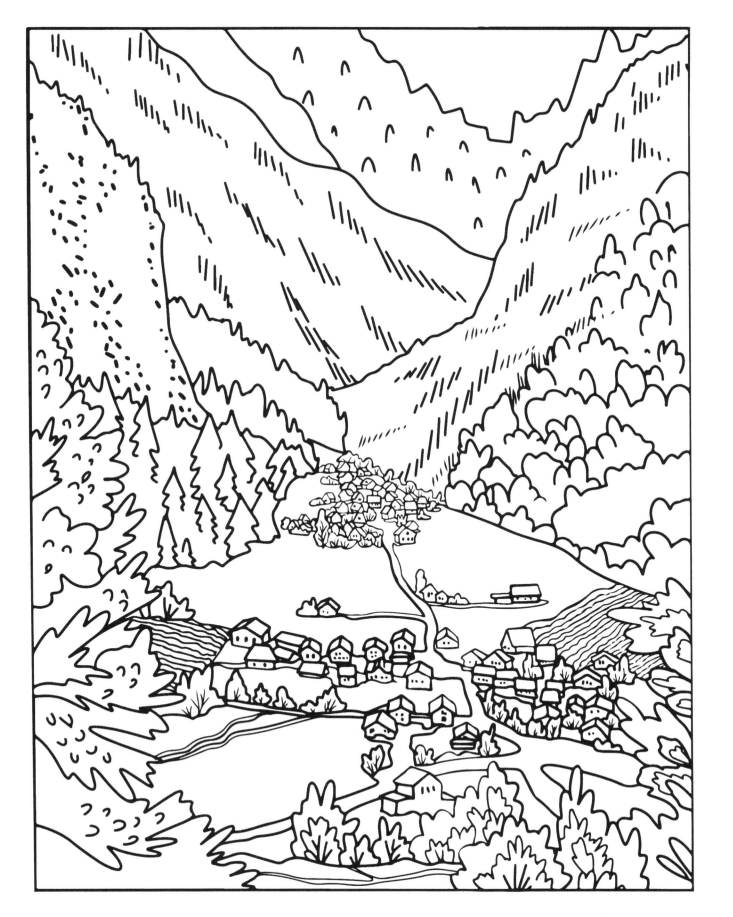

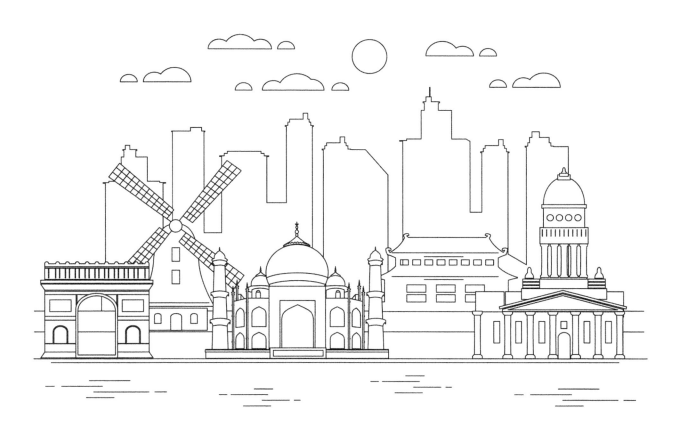

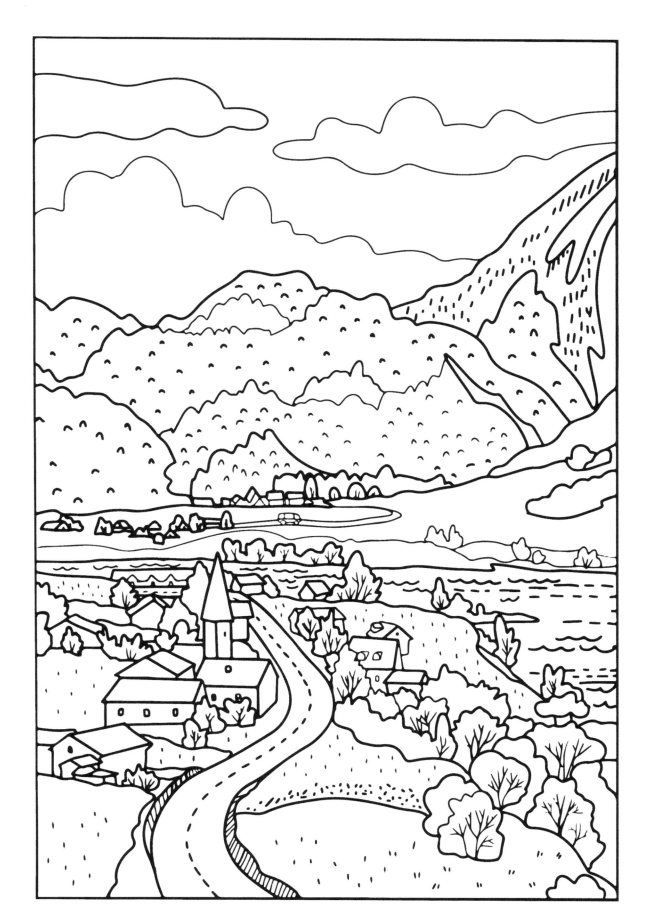

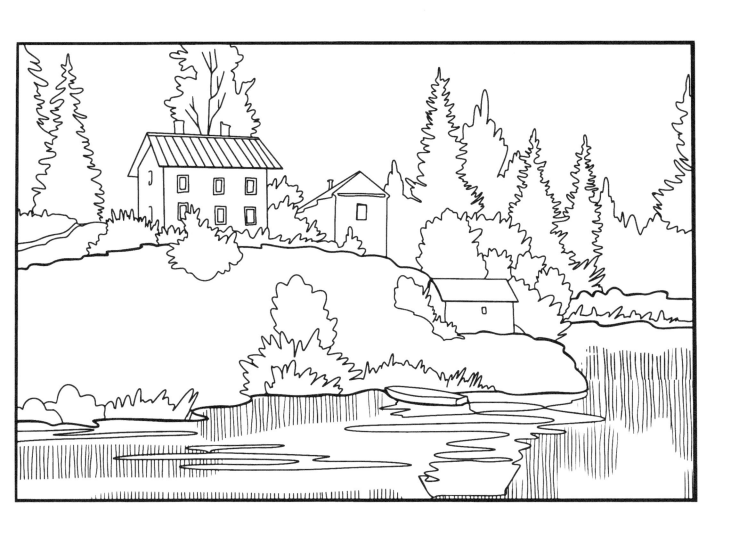

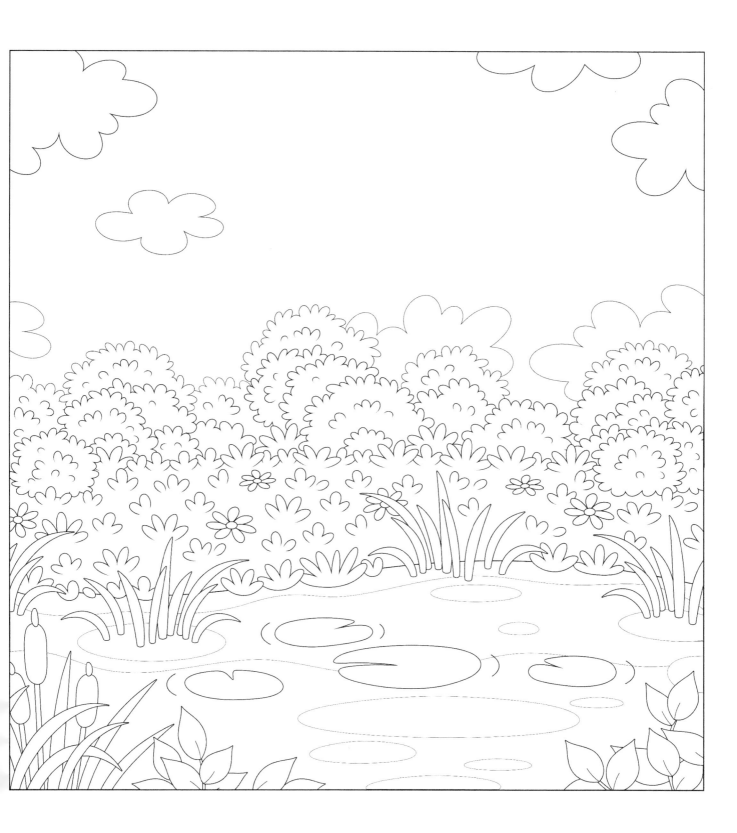

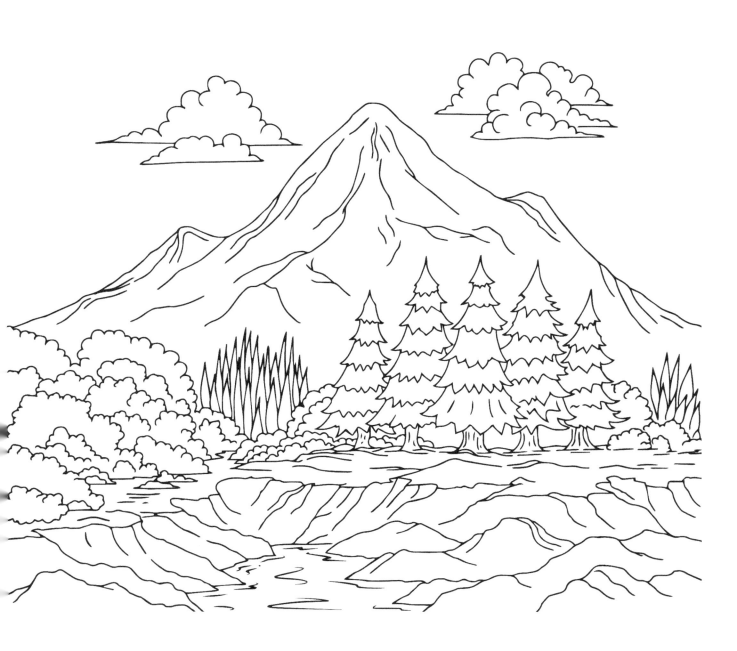

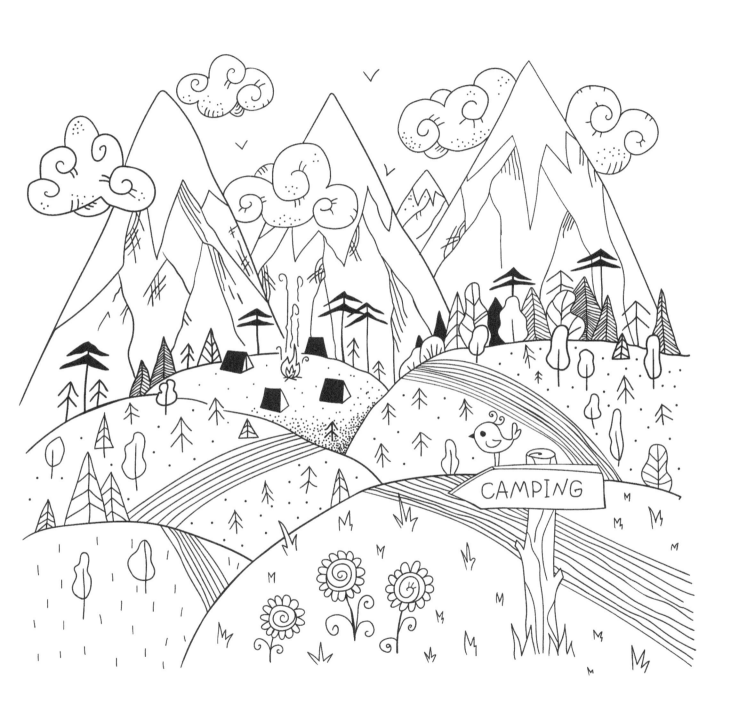

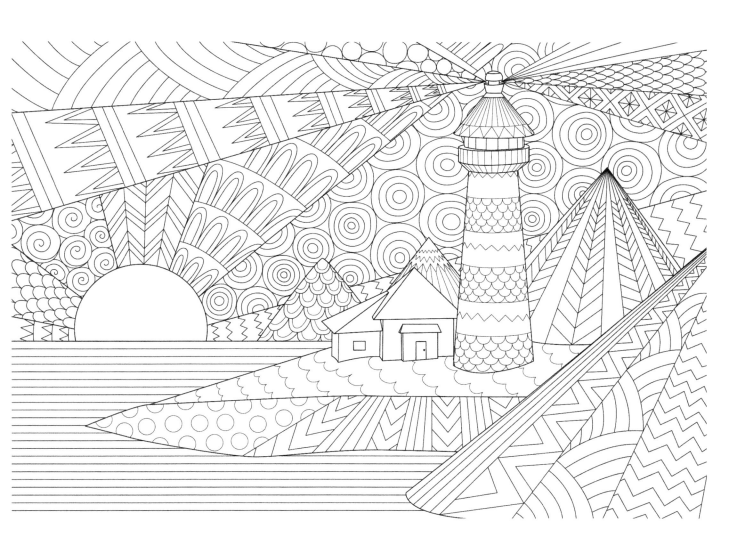

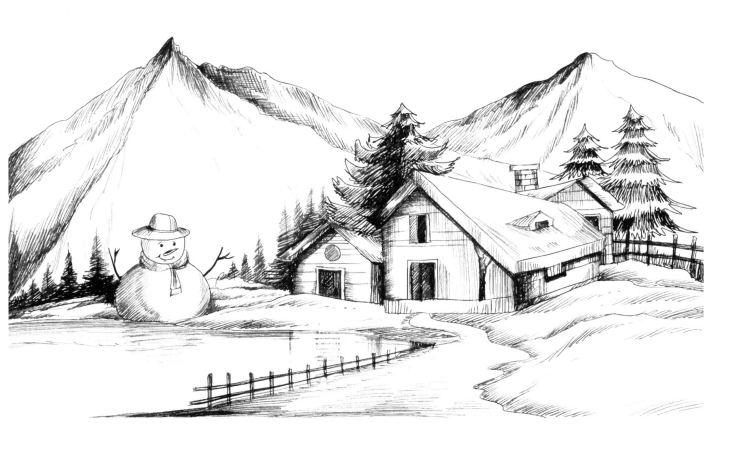

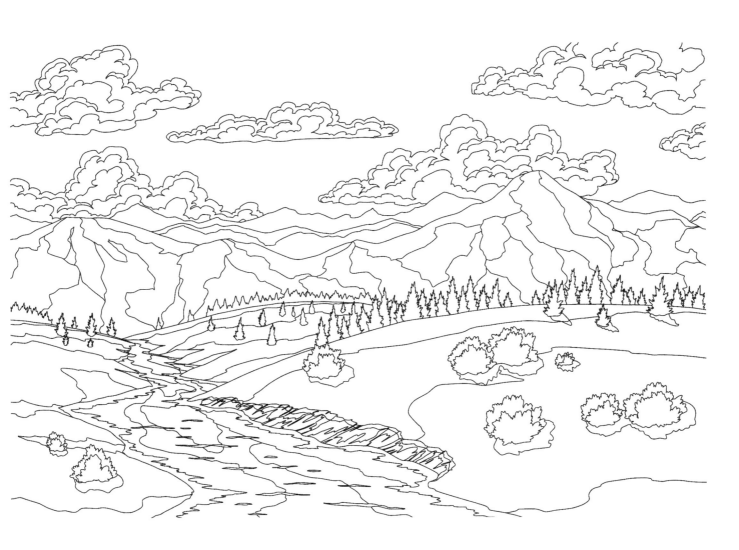

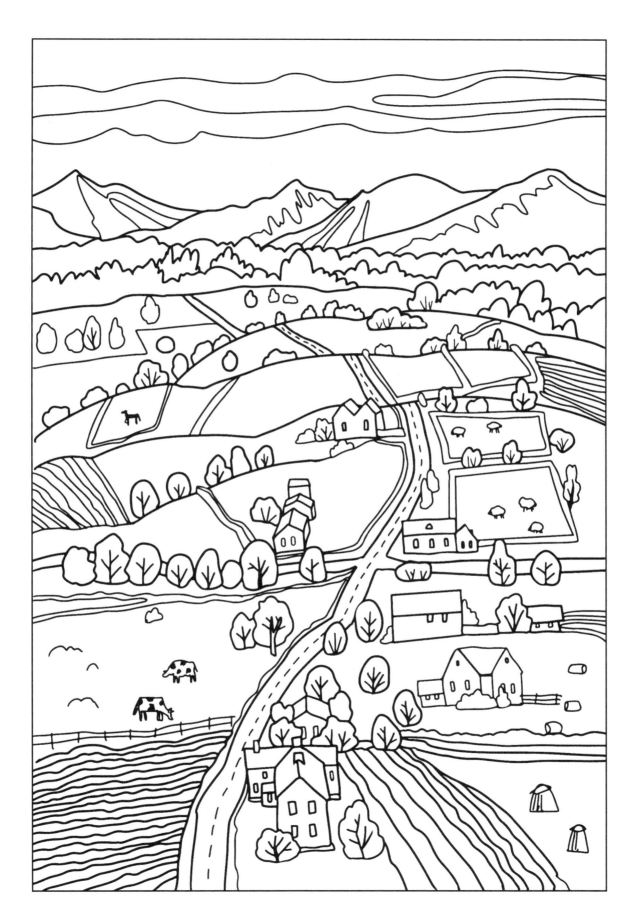

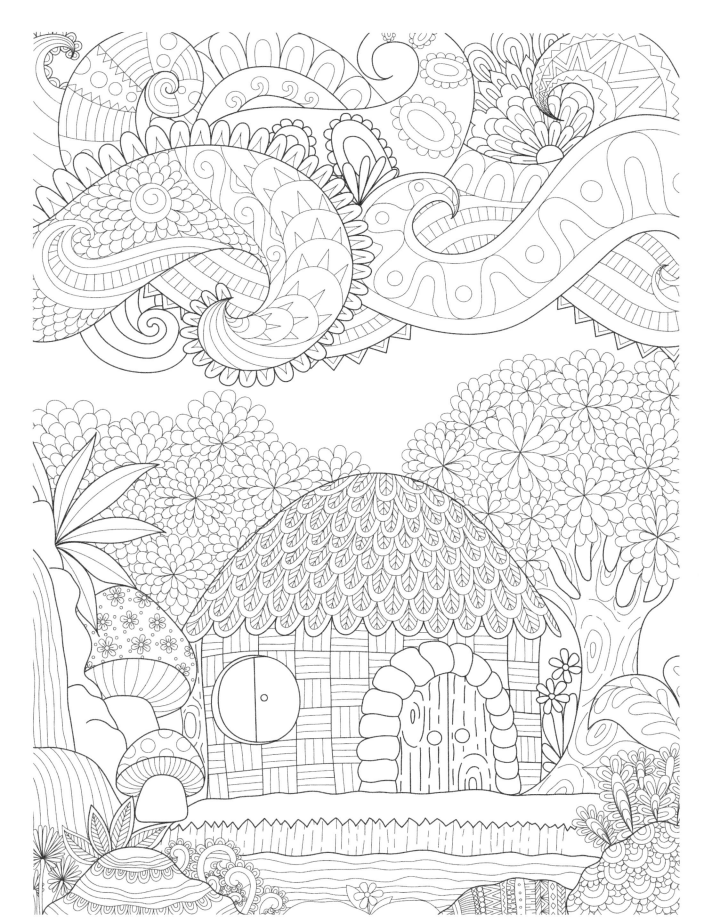

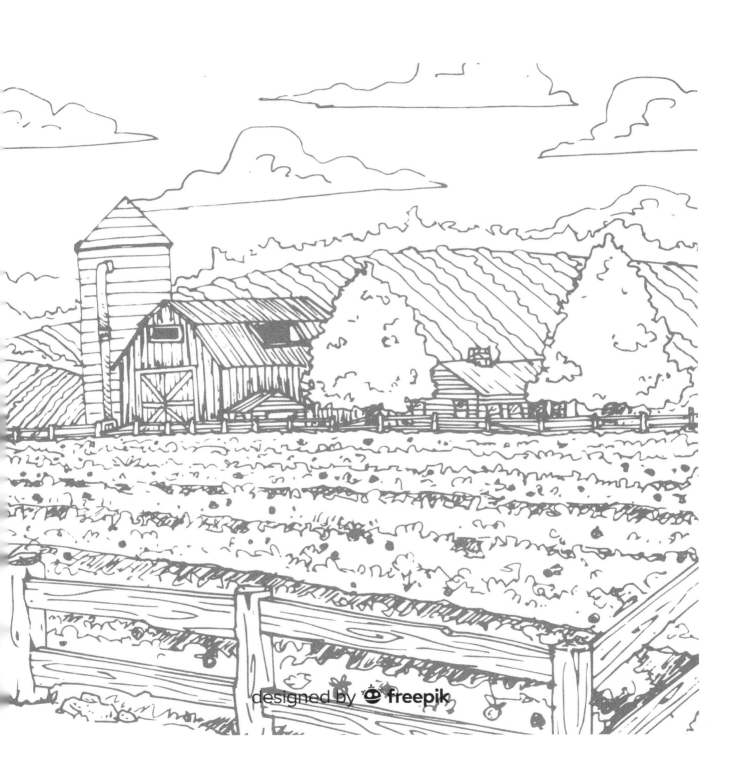

CPSIA information can be obtained
at www.ICGtesting.com
Printed in the USA
BVHW021139180423
662562BV00013B/640